M000086121

Burnout

The GOSPEL for REAL LIFE series

Brad Hambrick, Series Editor

Burnout

RESTING IN GOD'S FAIRNESS

BRAD HAMBRICK

P&R
PUBLISHING
P.O. BOX 817 • PHILLIPSBURG • NEW JERSEY 08865-0817

ISBN: 978-1-59638-662-4 (pbk)
ISBN: 978-1-59638-663-1 (ePub)
ISBN: 978-1-59638-664-8 (Mobi)

Printed in the United States of America

BOB CARES—OR AT LEAST HE USED TO. Bob cared about his family. He was actively involved with his children and felt disappointed whenever he couldn't regularly take his wife on a date. Bob cared about people—coworkers, fellow Christians in his small group, children, the homeless, and the lost overseas. Bob cared about his work. He was passionate about his career, advancing up the corporate ladder and wanting his reputation to be a good reflection of Christ. Everyone liked Bob and wanted to be like Bob. (P1)

"Caring" is a fire that burns, and burning fires require fuel. The problem was that the better Bob did at anything, the more everything came to him as a "great opportunity." Bob cared, so he tried to honor every "open door" God brought into his life. Soon there were more care-fires than there was Bob to burn, and he started to be consistently tired; not just physically tired, but mentally, emotionally, and spiritually tired. (P2)

Frequently Bob began to find that he didn't have "it" to give to his family, work, church, or friends. His talent and likability covered his feelings well enough that few people (other than his wife) noticed his lack of enthusiasm. But instead of taking this as a caution to slow down, Bob felt guilty that he wasn't able to give his best anymore, and he secretly began to wonder if he had risen above his actual ability in every area of life (if he could continue to be a good husband, good father, good manager, good small group leader, and so on). At first this guilt and shame provided a great energy boost and got him "back in the game." This happened several times over the course of a couple of years. He thought maybe it was a mild bout of depression or fatigue, so he started taking some vitamin supplements and trying to work out more often. That helped . . . for a while. (P3)

But the fatigue kept returning. Bob tried not to notice, but he could tell he was becoming more cynical. Bob was a caring guy who was starting not to care. He would help when needs arose, but doing so felt like a burden, and his once-tender heart toward others was growing callous. Now even the guilt he felt about not caring wasn't enough to jar him back into tenderhearted love. A sense of duty and not wanting to disappoint his family was all Bob had left. Strangely, this began to cause Bob to resent his family. As he realized this, he saw that he had already begun to avoid his friends. He reasoned that those who wanted him to be the old Bob just "don't understand me anymore and create too much pressure." He began to believe that only Bob was going to take care of Bob; everyone else would just take from him. (P4)

While Bob was going through the motions of work, home, and ministry (in that order of priority now), he was making sense of life in a whole new way. Life had become a black-and-white movie with a theme of duty and responsibility. Now anything that introduced color with freedom and excitement was deemed "good." Surprisingly, Bob kept wrestling with the fact that these things had all been deemed "bad" before—the attention from his secretary who was there to serve him and seemed to genuinely care, the couple of drinks at night that were faithful to take the edge off, and the impulse purchases that proved to Bob that he could do as he pleased. Bob's wife and "old friends" (as he now thought of them) raised concerns about these things. This only reinforced his now firmly held cynical belief that they didn't care about him and were judgmental, and pushed him further into isolation. (P5)

Predictably, Bob's work performance fell, his care for his secretary evolved into an affair, and the drinking grew beyond "a couple." During a two-month period his behavior started to come to light—his wife noticed the extra spending and found "questionable" (as she tried to politely called them) e-mails with the secretary, confronted him, persisted through his denials, and started to piece together the truth. With the separation that followed, the affair became public knowledge at work too. Within two more months Bob was fired, got a temp job, moved in an apartment with his secretary, was only able to see his kids for about an hour a week at McDonald's, and was under discipline at his church. When the dust settled, Bob was shocked and sickened. When he permitted himself to ask, "What happened?" his emotions fluctuated from intense shame-guilt to cold anger-bitterness and then retreated back into numb callousness. (P6)

How could he have gotten here? How could he have been as mean to his wife and friends as he was when his sin came to light? How could his conscience have missed that he was slipping into such dangerous patterns? He had taught classes at church on the dangers of everything he had done and gotten rave reviews about how good his insights were. Why was he just now beginning to care again? Now caring hurt so badly that he almost didn't want to come out of his cynical stupor, and when Bob talked to any of his "old friends," he found himself quickly getting defensive and retreating within his calloused conscience. (P7)

These questions are answered by the fact that Bob experienced burnout. This doesn't excuse any of the sins he committed, but it does mean that Bob started to place himself in "the danger zone" when his life looked good. The "time bomb was ticking" when it only looked like his "stock was rising." This means the changes Bob needed to make should have started in paragraph one, not paragraphs five or six.

QUESTION 1: WHAT IS BURNOUT?

Burnout is more than fatigue. When you're tired, a three-day weekend will improve your life. But when you are experiencing burnout, an extra day of rest won't cut the darkness anymore . . . even if you would allow yourself to take it.

Burnout is more than too much stress. When you're just stressed, completing a project or getting past a deadline creates a sense of relief and satisfaction. But when you are experiencing burnout, milestones don't satisfy like they did before; they get lost in the continual onslaught of "next."

Depression comes closer to capturing the experience of burnout. But depression is merely the absence of hope, and while it often involves isolation, it does not capture the level of cynicism or rebellious-escapism frequently associated with burnout.

It might be surprising, but more accurate, to think of burnout as a midlife crisis that can be experienced at any age. As burnout sets in, each dream and relationship that once promised life seems to be an emotional net loss even as it is fulfilled. Each accomplishment begins to feel like a mirage in the desert. The dry, draining heat of expectation and personal drive promises refreshment at the next milestone, but then vanishes as you approach it, only to be replaced by the next expectation with its new "promised mirage." The only way to protect yourself (it seems) is to become callous. Life requires you to still try, but life is cruel (as it becomes increasingly obvious).

With this said, burnout occurs when the things that we once relied upon for life and energy become a source of discouragement and a drain. Burnout occurs when we begin to live as if caring were a necessary enemy, and we begin to prefer the "living death" of numbness to "caring exhaustion" of Christian relationships and service. Whether we can articulate this poetic distinction or not, it becomes painfully obvious that our long-awaited and hard-worked-for hope cannot give us what it promised.

Let's go back and explore what happened with Bob.[1]

Paragraph One (Prerequisite: Caring)

Too often we think of burnout as a weakness instead of the result of an overdeveloped, underprotected strength. Those who

---

1. The outline of these materials is a gospel-tailored modification of the four-stage burnout progression observed by Mark Gorkin (contained in paragraphs three through six). A brief summary of his approach to the subject of burnout can be found at: http://www.stressdoc.com/four_stages_burnout.htm.

are not passionate about life do not experience burnout. We should all want to be burnout susceptible, because the alternative is directionless indifference toward the endless monotony of tasks life requires. This is not to make burnout the glorified "purple heart" of the Christian life, but to identify burnout as the temptation of choice for believers wanting to leave a mark on the world for God's kingdom in their sphere of influence with their God-given talents and gifts.

Paragraph Two (Unfocused or Unrealistic Discipline)

Every good opportunity is not from God or, at least, is not necessarily God's will for *your* life. Burnout is generally a struggle for the high-achieving person. They do good work, so their involvement is highly desired. This is affirming and, at first, energizing. However, with time, the fuel of affirmation becomes a drug. Affirmation (or other motives listed below) mutates from part of a healthy relationship diet to an internal parasite that insists on being fed before its host.

Paragraph Three (Fatigue)

Unrealistic discipline can only have one outcome—exhaustion. Good life management only delays the inevitable and increases the collateral damage when the crash comes. But fear and skill do not allow the crash to happen early in the process. The unsustainable life is prolonged in spite of the mental, emotional fatigue that mounts; ways are found to stimulate continued performance that does little to replenish life in the person serving. At the core, the person becomes more and more hollow while the exterior becomes more and more impressive and depended upon by others.

Paragraph Four (Motivation by Guilt or Shame)

It is easy to see how guilt and shame become the adrenaline button for someone marching toward burnout. Good things are happening. People are relying on him or her. God's kingdom is being advanced. The only thing that can interrupt this ideal circumstance, at least it seems, is the unwillingness of the burnout-in-waiting person to continue. When they stop doing, good stops happening, people are let down, and God's kingdom stalls (or so they think). This motivation "works," at least for a while. It simultaneously boosts the ego (pride) and lashes the conscience (guilt and shame). Both yield an artificial sugar-boost type of emotional energy. The problem is that the energy boost is void of any nutritional truths of the gospel, which nourish God's servant to a degree greater than his or her service drains.

Paragraph Five (Callousness and Cynicism)

When it feels as if God and others are manipulating you by your conscience, then the logical solution is to turn the conscience off. This conscience dimming is frequently accompanied by beginning to distance yourself from God (e.g., less prayer and Bible reading) and those who would want anything from you. While not addressing the larger life dynamics and heart issues, these changes are believed (if they are done intentionally) to be done as a healthy form of self-preservation. In actuality they are like the chemotherapy patient who stops his or her treatment for cancer because it seems to only make him or her sicker. In the case of isolation, we begin to solve the problem with a new and opposite form of exacerbation. The problem continues to get worse, but in the opposite direction, so we initially experience the progression of our malady as relief.

Paragraph Six (Failure and Crisis)

Not every case of burnout will be as morally dramatic as Bob's case study, but eventually the house of cards must fall. The fall may be moral, logistical, financial, or spiritual. But an unsustainable life will always break. The only questions are when, how, and with what consequences. The response of the cynical, calloused burned-out person is usually anger and defensiveness, but sometimes just despair. It makes sense to lash out against those who benefited from your excessive service and are now "pointing out" (regardless of tone or motive) the failure. "If they were really so 'concerned for me,' why didn't they notice the problem before I crashed?" The consequences of the failure or crash only serve to further enflame the deep sense of anger or despair. The size of their "opportunities and abilities" now becomes the size of their mess—one they feel utterly incapable to fix.

Paragraph Seven (Realization)

Once the dust settles from the frantic stage of failure and crisis, we begin to see that this was the inevitable outcome of the life we were trying to live. Those with adequate humility and reliance upon the gospel are able to embrace this realization. Those who are still trying to rely primarily upon self resist this realization because it creates the same guilt and shame that stoked the fires of their life toward burnout. If the gospel is embraced, then hope enters and begins to reinterpret the life that led to burnout in a way that makes service safe and enjoyable again. If the gospel does not transform the person's life (thinking and choices), then, at best, the person learns to manage life in a more functional but fearful way. Or, at worst, burnout is merely used as an emotionally forced time-out that serves to rejuvenate the person enough to start the cycle again.

QUESTION 2: WHAT CAUSES BURNOUT?

Burnout is never caused by a single area of life. Burnout is a function of our total life management. One area of life cannot get out of order without overt choices of neglect being made in other areas of life. This means that if we managed the other areas of our life well, we would have contained the area (e.g., work, ministry, parenting) that was the primary cause of burnout. We must resist the temptation to blame life, or even one area of our life management, for the experience of burnout. Burnout is a result of how we have managed our life as a whole.

So we might begin our assessment of burnout's cause with this foundational statement: burnout is the result of living beyond our means with the time God has provided. It is common to say that someone is living beyond their means financially. There is a cultural epidemic of people spending more than they earn. The majority of Americans have a negative net worth; they owe more than they own. We will use this parallel of financial and time management many times, so begin to think in these categories.

While financial insanity may be easier to track, time-management irrationality is probably even more pervasive and is an essential component to our financial folly. We must expect to pack more into life than is possible before we will try to force more into our budget than is possible. Our economy is based upon the exchange of time for money and money for stuff. Time is the primary commodity we spend and have expectations for. Money is only the currency (e.g., dollars) we have culturally agreed to use as a tangible expression of this value exchange. We pursue education and leverage our talents so that our time will become more monetarily valuable. But this masks the fact that the only thing we truly have to "spend" is our life.

Creating a Time Budget

So what value does it provide to boil burnout down to time management? It forces us to acknowledge the reality that we live within a 24-hour day, a 168-hour week, a 672-hour month (based on a four-week month), and an 8,760-hour year.

The next question is, What good does it do to know those numbers? If we believe God is fair (this is where an accurate functional theology is essential), then God's expectations of us fit within the time he has provided to us. Most of us do not live this way. We live with the driving mantra, "I have too much to do." We live as if this "too much" carries the moral weight of God's expectation (or at least the expectation of the "gods" we serve). We live as if God expects us to do every good thing that is asked of us and might benefit those around us.

It is easy for us to find 200 to 250 hours worth of good stuff to do in any given week—and that is without taking time to sin (which always takes or "robs" time). Honestly, the more Bible studies we attend and the better the preaching we sit under, the stronger this tendency becomes as we learn more of God's mission to reach the world through his church. This accounts for the tendency to isolate from Christian community. We begin to resist hearing anything else that we could do (but we always hear it as "should" do), because we have no mechanism to say no without guilt.

The first thing acknowledging God's fairness requires of us is to rest in the fact that everything God intends for us to do fits in a 168-hour week.[2] This means that even if there are 200 hours worth of excellent things to be accomplished in a week, we can have assurance that at least 32 hours of our agenda is outside the will of God for our life. This doesn't mean those activities are "outside the will of God" in terms of being bad, but that they are "outside the will of God" in the sense that if God wants to accomplish this, it will be done through someone other than us.

Budgeting Rest, Work, and Family

In order to think this way, you must have an intentional plan for using your time. Like a financial budget, it must be detailed enough to be useful, flexible enough to be practical, and looked at enough to alter your life. Let me begin by offering some general parameters for this time budget.[3] First, you

2. The time span of a week is chosen here because it is the most common and manageable unit of time for most people to think within. For those with a swing shift or other irregular weekly schedule it may be more beneficial to think within a monthly time frame.

3. "General parameters" does not mean one-size-fits-all. There are many factors that could alter these recommendations (e.g., chronic pain, having a disabled

should allocate at least 50 hours per week to sleep. This is a bare minimum of honoring the Sabbath command to express faith in God by resting a significant portion of each week, as Winston Smith reminds us.

> There is one very important reason to slow down and rest. God commands it. In fact, resting is so important that it is one of the Ten Commandments . . . God's command to rest forces us to acknowledge that God isn't just in perfect control of his world, but ours as well. Resting means acknowledging that our world really belongs to him and we must entrust our well-being into his hands.[4]

As we "set apart" this time (a phrase intentionally chosen from the Hebrew word for "holy"), it should be considered an application of offering our bodies as a "living sacrifice," worshiping God through accepting the limitations of being a finite creature (Rom. 12:1–2). This change may require a radical "renewing of the mind" for those who are moving toward burnout. It means acknowledging that *God honors our finiteness much more than we do.* Part of submitting to God's lordship over our life is to live within the limitations with which he created us.

Being finite is not the same as being selfish. For those who are motivated out of a sense of duty or people-pleasing, separating being finite and being selfish will be difficult. Accepting our limits is not the same as choosing our preferences over the preferences of others. By setting apart this time of minimal rest as "holy to the Lord" we are protecting ourselves and others. We must remember that we don't serve others well when we model

---

child/parent to care for, or providing as a single parent). The advice given is based upon the majority population's balanced life of sleep, work, relationships, service, and recreation.

4. Winston T. Smith, *Burned Out?: Trusting God with Your "To-Do" List* (Greensboro, NC: New Growth Press, 2010), 5, 9.

an unhealthy, imbalanced life as their leader. Winston Smith illustrates this in his own burned-out-Bob case study.

> Others avoided their responsibilities and relied on Bob instead of God. In effect, others were not growing because Bob[5] was in the way! Like an overindulgent parent, Bob unwittingly handicapped the people he tried to love because his goal was their respect and approval, not their maturity. He allowed people to depend on him instead of God.[6]

Second, you should budget around 50 hours per week for work. Even before the fall, God called every person to productively use his or her life for the betterment of others and stewardship of creation (Gen. 1:28). Allocating these hours may be easier for someone who works an hourly job than for those who are business owners, independent contractors, or full-time parents. But some limit must be put on this sector of life or our defeating motive (e.g., greed, ambition, people-pleasing, guilt, perfectionism) will expand this aspect of life until it destroys the others. When the rest of life is destroyed, productivity loses its purpose.

Third, you should budget at least 17 hours per week for marriage and family. This number is chosen a bit arbitrarily, but it represents a tithe (10 percent) of your time devoted to family.[7] Being part of a family will strongly influence your usage of time. This 17-hour time allotment is a recommended minimum amount of time to set aside for exclusive focus on family. If you

5. The "Bob" in Winston Smith's minibook is not the same "Bob" in the case study that began this material. But the same name was chosen to create consistency between different fictitious case studies.

6. Smith, *Burned Out?*, 19.

7. If you are single, then this time allotment should give you a minimal expectation of what kind of sacrifice should be expected when or if you marry. If you are married without children, then you need to realize the time you have devoted to marriage will begin to be split between spouse, child, and family as a whole.

are married with children, it would very difficult to have quality time with your family if this quantity of time is not being met.

"Family time" does not merely mean "in the same building at the same time." A useful definition of "family time" would be "investing my full attention in something that affirms my spouse or child by allowing me to know them better and making them feel more known by me." The type of activities that fit this description will vary widely based upon factors such as personality, interest, age, and season of life. The main point is that family time reinforces and strengthens the sense of knowing and being known within the family.

Budgeting "The Rest of Life"

Fourth, if you follow the recommendations above, that leaves 51 hours to be allocated for "the rest of life." The other parts of life should feel "holy" (set apart by God) before the week begins. In the first 117 hours of the week you are merely looking for the most wise and enjoyable way to accomplish rest, family time, and productivity. It is only these last 51 hours that we should feel an additional degree of freedom to use.

For many people this mindset will be uncomfortable, but when we call ourselves "God's servant" and claim to live "under the lordship of Christ," this necessarily places a limit upon our freedom. Within the first 117 hours we are free within the God-given role of finite creature, spouse-parent, and productive worker. Within the last 51 hours we are called to do maintenance, service, and recreation.

Maintenance. This involves cleaning one's home, mowing the yard, going to the grocery store, paying bills, and the other mundane activities necessary for life. In this area, a grandmother's advice on home cleanliness provides sound guidance for all areas of life maintenance: "A home should be clean enough to be healthy and messy enough to be happy."

Recreation. This involves the kind of activities you find rewarding and which replenish you in the mental, physical, and spiritual condition to serve God and others. Know yourself—what restores you, gives you energy, or relaxes you? Whatever these things are should be a regular part of your schedule.

Service. This involves service through your church to the congregation and community for the purpose of spreading the gospel to the ends of the earth and deeper into the lives of those around you. The discussion that follows will focus primarily upon this area since that is the particular area of life that this booklet is designed to prevent from becoming a contributor to burnout.

No recommended percentages or time allotments can be given for these three areas. But it should be noted that all three are essential to healthy living and should be given time. Healthy relationships are those that actively help you guard and honor balance in all three of these areas.

To help you assimilate what we have covered to this point, let's return to the parallel of a financial budget. A good financial budget should divide various expenses into four types:

1. **Fixed Necessity:** These are expenses that are essential for living (necessity) and are the same each month (fixed). This category would include mortgage, insurance premiums, or minimum debt payments.
2. **Variable Necessity:** These are expenses that are essential for living (necessity) and are not the same each month (variable). This category would include groceries, gasoline, or the power bill.
3. **Fixed Luxury:** These are expenses that are not essential for living (luxury) and are the same each month (fixed). This category would include various memberships, cable packages, or nonessential monthly subscriptions.

4. **Variable Luxury:** These are expenses that are not essential for living (luxury) and are not the same each month (variable). This category would include food prepared in a restaurant, irregular entertainment expenses, and clothing beyond basic attire.

In a normal family budget, necessity expenses (categories one and two) will comprise 75 to 80 percent of the total income. This means that we only make monthly decisions about 20 to 25 percent of our income (that is, *if* we have made wise choices about our expenses). The rest was decided in our necessary life commitments (and debts). Similarly, the majority of our time usage will fit under the category of "necessity" (the first 117 hours that are God's minimums for healthy living), and with the minority we have greater personal discretion (the last 51 hours spent based on the "luxury" of personal preference within God's design and mission).

The financial budget example is particularly helpful for this last 51 hours. A good financial budget seeks to balance fixed luxury and variable luxury spending. If the luxury spending is skewed towards fixed expenses, then it will lack the flexibility necessary to be practical. When all fun is planned fun, there is no room for life, and you'll either break or resent the budget. If the luxury spending is skewed toward variable expenses, then it will likely lack the balance necessary to capture the interest of the family as a whole. Each month members will battle for "their things," and the budget will become a battleground rather than a document of peace.

Side note: Often a life headed toward burnout will result from the absence of a wise budget. The more expenses we take on, the more time we must sacrifice to acquire that money. Eventually we spend ourselves to the point that we must work into burnout to meet our financial commitments.

Generosity vs. Sacrifice

The notion of variable and fixed luxury spending with finances forces us to ask what categories we should use in dividing these last 51 hours. Variable and fixed are useful, but I believe there is a more basic distinction to introduce first: generosity and sacrifice. It is admitted that the distinctions made here are tailored to the purposes of this booklet and are not inherent within the words themselves. But if burnout is to be avoided, this distinction is essential, regardless of what terminology is used to label it.

Generosity: planning to give more of the last 51 hours to serving God and others than we are comfortable doing, and learning to find our joy in this service. C. S. Lewis makes this point about finances:

> I am afraid the only safe rule is to give more than we can spare. In other words, if our expenditure on comforts, luxuries, amusements, etc., is up to the standard common among those with the same income as our own, we are probably giving away too little. If our charities [giving habits] do not at all pinch or hamper us, I should say that they are too small. There ought to be things we should like to do and cannot do because our charities [giving] expenditure excludes them.[8]

This time allotment should be worked into our general time budget. Generosity, like luxury spending, should be balanced between two types.

1. **Fixed-"Planned" Generosity:** These are commitments within your last 51 hours (generosity) that require regular— daily, weekly, or monthly—participation (fixed). These

8. C. S. Lewis, *Mere Christianity* (New York: HarperSanFrancisco, 2001), 81–82.

commitments should be in your areas of passion and gifting to ensure that your regular, ongoing service is a source of life for you in addition to blessing others. These commitments should only be accepted after a review of your time budget and in consultation with your family. Fixed commitments should not comprise the totality of your generosity time.

2. **Variable-"Spontaneous" Generosity:** These are commitments within your last 51 hours (generosity) that are one-time events or only require periodic involvement (variable). These commitments usually arise from the needs of your family, friends, small group, or church at large. You should have time designated (this means creating a lifestyle in which you are able to be available) for responding to the needs of those around you.

Sacrifice: cutting into the first 117 hours for crisis needs. This type of activity should be relatively rare because it is unsustainable. Sacrifice is good only when it is sacrifice and not a way of life. Generosity is as close as sacrifice can get to a way of life and remain healthy. The financial parallel is again helpful. It is foolish to give the money for your house payment to pay someone else's mortgage. You are simply trading foreclosures. When you dip into the first 117 hours, you are tapping into what God has said is required to live healthy. To tap into this on a regular basis is not a virtue (an act of faith in God), but either an act of pride (believing you are the exception) or fear (being blinded by circumstance to God's design for life). When sacrifice is made, it should be done (1) in consultation with a community of trusted Christian friends; (2) in concert with the efforts of one's church; and (3) only on a defined, short-term basis.

The Example of Moses and Jethro

Much has been said about time management, its influence upon burnout, and how we should approach the subject. But we must admit there are few places in Scripture where the subject is addressed directly. One of the places where time management and burnout are addressed most directly is Exodus 18, where Jethro observes how Moses, his son-in-law, was trying to manage his responsibilities with the children of Israel.

His words, which were recorded in Scripture as an example to follow (making them more than good advice from an old man), provide an invaluable principle:

> Moses' father-in-law said to him, "*What you are doing is not good. You and the people with you will certainly wear yourselves out*, for the thing is too heavy for you. You are not able to do it alone. Now obey my voice; I will give you advice, and God be with you! You shall represent the people before God and bring their cases to God, and you shall warn them about the statutes and the laws, and make them know the way in which they must walk and what they must do. Moreover, look for able men from all the people, men who fear God, who are trustworthy and hate a bribe, and place such men over the people as chiefs of thousands, of hundreds, of fifties, and of tens. And let them judge the people at all times. Every great matter they shall bring to you, but any small matter they shall decide themselves. So it will be easier for you, and they will bear the burden with you. If you do this, God will direct you, *you will be able to endure*, and all this people also will go to their place in peace." So Moses listened to the voice of his father-in-law and did all that he had said. (Ex. 18:17–24)

Most often this passage is used to teach the importance of delegation. That is an accurate application of this passage and one that is relevant to the subject of burnout. But in light of the discussion of this material, there is a principle that comes before the application to delegation—*if something becomes a way of life and is not sustainable, then it is not "good," no matter how "necessary" it may be.*

Moses was solving disputes for people who had no problem-solving skills—their people had been slaves and lived by a master's orders for four hundred years. Moses was, humanly speaking, responsible for them being in this newfound dilemma of freedom. Moses was doing a good job, as best we can tell, at making good laws and rulings. Obviously people liked what he had to say; they kept coming to him for advice. It was all good because it was effective, and it was all bad because it was not sustainable.

To use the language and categories we have developed, Moses was going past being generous with his last 51 hours and was beginning to regularly sacrifice his first 117 hours. Someone in Moses' inner circle, who could see what was happening and who cared enough to speak, spoke up. It was life changing. Moses, who got handwritten messages from God on a mountaintop, thought it profound enough to record in his book. Actually, it was his passion for the message and mission Moses received from God on the mountaintop that blinded him to the burnout he was barreling towards.

It is on the basis of this principle of sustainability that the generosity-sacrifice distinction is made. Generosity within a well-planned and monitored life is sustainable. Occasional sacrifice within a well-planned and monitored life is sustainable. When we do not have a well-planned and monitored life, then our service to God runs the risk of degenerating into "reckless giving" in "blind faith" to "emotionally compelling" situations without defined limits on our ability to give. When we fail to account for sustainability, serving eventually consumes the servant.

Making a Time Budget

If we do not begin to put pen to paper, then all of this will be nothing more than good intentions and fancy talk. Crunching numbers is only the first step toward application, but it is a necessary step. The number-crunching phase will come in two parts. First, we must examine how we currently live. How many hours are we trying to cram into a 168-hour week? As we see this, it will allow the adrenaline, fatigue, and guilt we feel to make more sense. Second, we must prayerfully consider how God would have us divide our 168-hour week during this season of life.

The tool on the next two pages is designed to help you make this assessment using the categories and approach that have been outlined in this material.[9] The first page is a sample time budget for someone describing their life "as is." You will quickly notice that the budget is 25 hours overdrawn before anything has a chance to go wrong during a "real" week. This person wrote their schedule based upon a weekly schedule and only used the monthly column for nonweekly activities (e.g., taking a two-hour date with their spouse every other week).

When using a chart like this, you cannot itemize everything you do. This is especially true for those who have the spiritual gift of multitasking. Notice that things like "general chores" are lumped together as one line item. In order to actually apply a budget like this, you will likely need to list some of the core functions of your time budget (e.g., Wednesday is laundry day; Friday is grocery day; every other Saturday is date night).

Another essential mind-set change will involve your family's beginning to think as a collective unit (we), instead of a collection of individuals (me). Family schedules do not exist as independent islands. Most commitments made by each family member affect the schedules of the other family members. This other-mindedness creates excellent discipleship moments with the children and may be the most effective premarital counseling your children ever receive.

9. This tool is modified and adapted from a similar resource created by James Petty and found in his book *Step by Step: Divine Guidance for Ordinary Christians* (Phillipsburg, NJ: P&R Publishing, 1999), 272–75.

Step 1. To become familiar with this tool, write in the far-right column changes you would suggest to this person if he were a friend who asked you for advice on living within a realistic schedule. As you do this, you will realize afresh that living within a realistic schedule means cutting some "good" things. Starting with a generic example should help you get ready to do this with your personal life.

Step 2. Complete a time budget based upon the time commitments that you currently try to fulfill. PDF copies of the time budget form can be found at www.bradhambrick.com/burnout. It may take three to four weeks of observing yourself before you are confident that you have an accurate representation of what you're trying to accomplish. But start by getting your best guess on paper, and then revise it as you observe yourself throughout the next couple of weeks.

Step 3. Makes notes about where changes are needed, and begin discussing them with family and friends who will be affected. If you try to make changes in your personal life without talking to those whose lives will be influenced, then you are setting up conflict that will either aggravate your sense of guilt or the tendency to isolate from those who "don't care about or understand you." Both tendencies will fuel burnout and are likely a product of their ignorance of the problem more than their entrenched demands upon you.

Step 4. Put your revised and realistic time budget on paper. This is not a for-all-time document. If it lasts for six months, you will be fortunate. But having a working copy of where you are now will allow you to make effective changes as life evolves, without having to read through material like this again. The work you have done to this point will serve you well, even when your current time budget is completely obsolete.

Time Budget (Sample)

Activities	Type				Time		Changes Needed
List All Your Activities	Essential	Energy Giving	Energy Taking	Planned Generosity	Hours Required in 7 days (168)	Hours Required in 28 Days (672)	**How to Make Needed Changes**
Nightly Sleep			x		49		Start with 50/week or 200/month
Family							Minimum 17 hours/week
Meals together (10 per week)	x	x			5		
Family devotions	x	x			3		
Attend/serve church together	x	x			2		
Play time with kids	x		x		7		
Date night	x	x			1	4	
Time with spouse	x	x			7		
Work							
Base work hours	x				40		
Commute to/from work	x				10		
Overtime			x		5		
Side jobs for extra $			x		5		
Maintenance							
Getting ready for the day	x		x		5		
Exercise			x		3		
House repairs & yard work	x		x		1	4	
General chores	x		x		4		
Doing the budget	x		x		0.5		
Recreation							
Sleeping in or nap	x	x			2		
Pesonal devotions	x	x			3.5		
Sports league		x			2		
Watching television					14		
Ministry							
Lead small group	x	x		x	2		
Preparation for small group	x		x	x	1		
Other ministry		x		x	2		
Spontaneous generosity			x		3		If no time put here, then always "in the way"
Other							
Talking to parents		x			2		
Kids' sporting events			x		5		
Miscellaneous					9	35	5% for general inefficiency of life
	Total Time I've Planned				193		
	Time God Has Provided				168	672	

Time Budget (Blank)

Activities	Type				Time		Changes Needed
List All Your Activities	Essential	Energy Giving	Energy Taking	Planned Generosity	Hours Required in 7 days (168)	Hours Required in 28 Days (672)	**How to Make Needed Changes**
Nightly Sleep							Start with 50/week or 200/month
Family							Minimum 17 hours/week
Work							
Maintenance							
Recreation							
Ministry							
Spontaneous generosity							If no time put here, then always "in the way"
Other							
Miscellaneous					9	35	5% for general inefficiency of life
	Total Time I've Planned						
	Time God Has Provided				168	672	

Motives for Burnout

Now that we have been practical, let's be honest. We did not get to the brink of burnout (or over the cliff) because we lacked an itemized time-budgeting tool. Tools won't ultimately tame what got us into this mess. They may show us the mess and the changes that are necessary. When we are worn down and desperate (humble), we will acknowledge what we see and change (repent). But once we get strong (prideful) again, we will think we can "handle it" (foolishness), unless our reason for change runs deeper than a time budget (penetrates our heart).

That is the purpose of this section—to help us see why we got here, so that we can address the root cause of burnout (heart sins) instead of merely its primary manifestation (an unrealistic schedule). Changes at this level will be more challenging than changing your schedule, but the freedom you experience from these changes will be more liberating as well.

Below are nine motives that commonly contribute to burnout. As you read them, you'll find that they are not mutually exclusive. Your goal is to see and hear yourself. You have likely accepted the mind-set of these nine motives as "the way things are" without seeing them as the destructive forces (sin) that push you away from restful dependence upon God in the midst of work.

Pride. "I want it to be done right." "I am the only one who can do [blank]." There may be some limited, useful truth in these statements. God does uniquely gift and equip people for certain tasks. But if we find this mind-set encompassing more and more of our life, it is probably the mark of territorial pride rather than the outflow of our gifting. When God's gifts are used as God intended, they multiply the number of available leaders rather than merely elevating (and thereby exhausting) the one whom God gifted.

As we consider pride and burnout, it is important to reflect on how the fall and God's subsequent curse on the human race affected our work. Winston Smith observes: "Complicating matters, when God confronted Adam and Eve, he cursed the very things in which men and women would find their worth: he cursed their labor . . . You may try to take pride in your work; you may try to find life and meaning in your children, but God isn't going to make it easy for you."[10]

Pride does not have to say, *I can do this better.* It can merely say, *I can make this my life.* When understood this way, God's curse on Adam and Eve was merely a form of protection. Before the fall, self-sufficiency and autonomy were not temptations. After the fall, people needed to be protected from these temptations because of the incredible gift of reason that came with being made in the image of God. God made work and relationships hard so that it would be harder for us to be satisfied with them apart from him—and easily wander toward an eternity separated from God.

Pride can also show itself in the attitude that says, *I don't want people messing up my little world.* We make a world that meets our specifications. We look at our world and pronounce it "good." Then we fight to keep the "outside forces of evil" from corrupting our world. People are invited to live in our world as long as they obey the rules of our world. The problem is that we were made only to manage God's world, not to create our own. So this form of pride inevitably leads to the exhaustion of burnout.

Fear. This is burnout built on the prefix "What if . . . ?" If your life is driven into the ground by trying to brace against an endless stream of hypothetical situations that are limited only by the creativity of your pessimistic imagination, then burnout will be the only periodic relief you experience from your "normal" life of fear.

The hypotheticals we create can be about external circumstances (e.g., What if my children forget to wash their hands before eating, get sick, miss a week of school, fall behind in sec-

10. Smith, *Burned Out?*, 22.

ond grade, begin to feel not smart enough, underperform through high school, do not get into the college of their choice, marry a second-class spouse, get a job they don't enjoy, get divorced, and I never get to see my grandchildren?). Or the hypotheticals can be related to our internal capabilities, as described by Winston Smith: "Bob lived out of a sense of shame and inadequacy that had dogged him his entire life. In his heart, Bob considered himself a failure and a fraud. He lived as if it were just a matter of time until he was exposed as a failure at every level. His busyness was a failed attempt to address a problem with who he was as a person."[11]

Fear can result in being overprotective or overachieving, but a life ruled by fear is not sustainable and will inevitably result in burnout. Unless we begin to trust (the verb-form opposite of fear) God, we will not experience peace or rest (the noun-form opposites of fear). Without trust in God, life becomes an endless cycle of burnout (usually called depression in this cycle), in which our body recuperates and prepares for another round of fear-living.

Approval / Fear of Man. "I'm not happy unless you're happy." This is the motto of codependent burnout. In this approach to relationships we become so close to someone that their mood becomes the emotional ceiling for our mood. It feels wrong to enjoy life or have a greater level of contentment than anyone we care about. Loving becomes a draining and limiting thing to do.

Another form of this approach to burnout is the "guess why you're not happy game," while assuming the answer is always "something I did" or "something I should have done." The exhausting premise of this approach to relationships is that if I love you well (i.e., fill your love tank or meet your needs), then you should be happy. All unhappiness in those I care about becomes a personal indictment (i.e., my fault).

11. Ibid., 20.

This illusion of control that would allow me to create a relational utopia becomes an immense burden when life won't play by the simplistic rules I have assumed or been taught. Rather than questioning my theory of relationships, I just keep trying harder (sound like fatigue?). At least until I get angry (sound like callous and cynical?) that I am trying harder than my spouse and friends (sound like withdrawal and setting up for a crisis?).

Escapism from Being Still. "I just don't like to be still. I want to do something." Our bodies and minds were not made for perpetual stimulation. In the absence of being still we lose the opportunity to evaluate life, learn from our mistakes, and discern God's calling on our life. The result is a series of random (at best) or foolish (at worst) choices that result in our activity getting us nowhere. When we finally realize that our effort is not achieving anything, life begins to feel pointless, and burnout sets in.

If this motive fits you, an important question to ask is, What am I avoiding by being busy? It may be that busyness is a form of penance that allows you to forget about your self-defined "big" sin rather than embracing God's forgiveness. Or it may be that busyness is a way to distract yourself from the absence of any clear life direction. You just do a lot, especially for God. Whatever you avoid by busyness, know that being honest with God and Christian friends about it will be more productive than being busy, and it is the only way off the burnout cycle.

Some people are perpetually busy, but only secondarily as a form of escape. They just love the "new" and hate boredom. If this is you, then an important point to remember is that reflection is the completion of a joy. It is reflection that contextualizes a joy as a part of God's blessing and prepares the joy to be shared so that it blesses others. When we move incessantly from one pleasure to another, we are consuming our pleasures in a self-centered way (even if they are group/social pleasures) that does not allow us to use these blessings as God intends—as a way to love God and love others.

Over-Reliance upon Order and Neatness. "I just know how I like things and have a hard time resting until they are 'just so.'" In this scenario we find our rest in our surroundings rather than God's care and provision. We confuse God for being a God of order with order being our god. It would be easy to write off this motive to only those who are obsessive-compulsive, but while OCD would result in this form of burnout, it is inaccurate to think that only a struggle of clinical significance can result in burnout.

In this approach to life we only allow ourselves to rest when life is mastered (defined by whatever measure to which we assign the most value—keeping a clean house, being ahead of the work schedule, assuring the children's academic performance, being on pace for retirement, and so on). While we would probably argue otherwise, our standard of order or neatness becomes its own system of works-based righteousness. We may still rely on Christ for heaven and think his ways are the best ways to achieve what we must have. But we have defined what we "must have" for ourselves, and emotionally respond to everything else (heaven, godly character, etc.) as if it is secondary. We are still the ones "making happen" what is most important in our lives, even if we choose to use God's ideas to get there.

As with anything we try to do in our strength, we eventually realize that our own strength is insufficient, and exhaustion gives way to burnout. This is the inevitable trap of any works-righteousness approach to life. Age, ambition, human error, or other factors related to living in a fallen world, create a scenario in which we cannot keep "the standard" anymore. We care too much to lower the standard, so we strive until we give out or rely on God for the strength we never had.

Guilt. "I do good things because I've been bad. I do good things to avoid feeling bad." In this approach to motivation we live life as God's servants without equally living as God's dearly loved children. It becomes hard to celebrate achievement or even take restful contentment in a job well done because life is viewed as a punishment-aversion game. We think about what we are avoiding as much, if not more, than what we are pursuing.

Acceptable pleasures begin to illicit feelings of guilt. Spending money and taking time off are judged through the lens of guilt. You may sincerely want nice things for others and for them to have the time to enjoy them, but enjoying them yourself feels wrong. Recharging activities bear the emotions of judgment, even if you place no overt regulation against them.

When others praise you for your high level of accomplishment and upstanding character, it is easy to begin to mistake their praise for your actions as confirmation for the value system that drives them. This slowly moves your "biggest fans" into the crowd of condemning voices. When you feel like you need a break, you replay their praise as reasons to drive on. Again, the isolation and callousness of burnout become the only "logical" response within this value system.

"Addicted to My Level of Productivity." This phrase is taken from Tim Keller as he reflected on his early years of church planting and its effects on himself personally and his marriage.[12] Progress can be the best of drugs. Unlike other drugs or addictive habits, the lie "It's not hurting anybody else" is true with progress. More than not hurting anybody, progress is a blessing to so many people, especially progress in ministry.

Progress begins to make "normal" feel "negative." Moments that bear nothing "significant" begin to be measured against those when something "significant" is accomplished (even if the comparison is unintentional). The sensation makes normal feel

12. Tim and Kathy Keller, *The Meaning of Marriage: Facing the Complexities of Commitment with the Wisdom of God* (New York: Dutton Adult, 2011), 146.

like a letdown. Contentment begins to be graded on a curve, and the curve is above-average productivity.

In yet another way, rest is robbed of its restfulness. When satisfaction requires a reason, then all of life becomes performance-driven again, like it was before we experienced the liberty of the gospel. Addiction (the word here used descriptively, not clinically) to productivity reintroduces a blended form of the motives of pride, fear, and guilt; the pride of an elevated self-standard and the fear-guilt that comes with the thought of not meeting that standard.

Unnecessary "Necessary" Pleasure. "I am willing to work hard to enjoy nice things in life. I want to live a full life and experience all that God has to offer." For this person, burnout comes through using work as a means to an end and living for the end. Work gets me all the toys and trips, and I am driven enough by the toys and trips to exhaust myself.

This one can be hard to identify because there are usually many "recharging activities" in this person's schedule. Actually he or she is overcharged. Like the battery for the remote-control truck we got my son for Christmas and left charging until Valentine's Day (you can tell how much he wanted the truck), the charging killed the battery. A solid work ethic and an equally active "inner child" leave little room for rest.

This motive is particularly prevalent in child-centered families or immature adults (oddly, very different personalities walking a similar path to burnout). In both cases a balanced life is exchanged for the best memories (although the immature adult may just call them "stories"). Sustainability is silenced in the name of "we will only get to live once," and that one life is crippled by its own nearsighted mathematics.

Perfectionism. "If it's worth doing, it's worth doing right. When I put my name on something, I want it to mean something. It just bothers me to half do something." The phrase "good enough" begins to feel like a deal with the devil. Actually, if the devil cannot get us to accept bad, then he's glad to get us so consumed with good that we self-destruct. That is what happens to the perfectionist who burns out.

One often undetected way that perfectionism leads to burn-out is when we reduce our world to the size of things we do well. There is great wisdom in engaging tasks or relationships that we do poorly. I have labeled these activities "the spiritual discipline of awkwardness." These are active, emotional reminders that we live by grace. When we only engage in activities that we do well or interact with people with whom we share common interests, then we often lose an experiential sense of how much we live by grace.

Perfectionism, when lived out, creates a sense of power and pride. When we are recognized as "the standard" in our field by our peers, we cease to have a healthy sense of living under God's law. We become the law, the standard to which others strive. If we maintain self-awareness, this is a fearful thing that drives us and leads us to burnout as described under "the fear of man." If we begin to believe our own fairy tale, then superhuman living will inevitably crash any human soul as described under "pride."

Other. These nine motives and descriptions are not exhaustive. The motive that leads you to burnout may be different, or the expression of one of these motives may take a form not described above. The purpose of these materials is to provide an example of how to see and hear yourself. Take time to write your motives and their key expressions.

_____

_____

_____

_____

_____

_____

_____

_____

_____

QUESTION 3: HOW CAN I PREVENT BURNOUT?

Not everyone who reads this material is in the midst of burnout; some are concerned counselors and friends, others know burnout is a struggle they need to guard against. This final section is meant to provide preventative tips and early warning signs for burnout. Some of these pieces are reminders summarizing what you've learned in this material, while others are new ideas.

Start the day in relaxed dependence. This is merely a new description for "quiet time" or "personal devotions." This description focuses on the state of being (relaxed dependence) rather than the activity (reading, praying, or journaling). Both the state of being and activity are essential. For those struggling with burnout the temptation can be to make your time with God one more self-improvement activity, rather than a place of refuge and time of rest.

Steward your finite body—eat healthy, exercise, and sleep. You have a responsibility before God to care for your body in a way that places you in the best position to face life's struggles. You do not want to put yourself in an avoidable situation where your spirit is willing but your flesh is weak (Matt. 26:41).

Live within your 168-hour week. This concept helps you remember that when you say yes to a new thing, you must say no to something you are currently doing.

Practice stillness. Schedule some time daily to be still—not doing a task, watching television, listening to music, or responding to conversation. Use this as a tangible reminder that you can stop and the world won't fall off its axis.

Practice the spiritual discipline of awkwardness. Enjoy engaging in tasks or conversations which you have not mastered. Let these times be an affirmation from God that he loves you as you are and that your performance does not increase or decrease God's love for you.

Learn how to manage stress and conflict. Two of the leading predictors of burnout are stress and conflict. If these are areas you feel particularly uncomfortable with or ill prepared to face, then study them during your personal reading time.[13]

Receive adequate training for major life responsibilities. Another major predictor of burnout is inadequate training for major responsibilities. If you do not feel adequately equipped for a significant responsibility, seeking training in this area would be a wise investment in your time budget.

Have nonfunctional friendships. It is important to have friends who don't relate to you on the basis of a title or position. When all your friends know you because you are their teacher, parent, boss, pastor, colleague, supplier, and so on, you are setting yourself up for burnout.

13. On anxiety you might read Elyse Fitzpatrick, *Overcoming Fear, Worry, and Anxiety* (Eugene, OR: Harvest House Publishers, 2001) or Edward Welch, *Running Scared: Fear, Worry, and the God of Rest* (Greensboro, NC: New Growth Press, 2007).

On conflict it would be advised that you read Ken Sande, *The Peacemaker: A Biblical Guide to Resolving Personal Conflict*, 3rd ed. (Grand Rapids, MI: Baker Books, 2004) or Ken Sande with Tom Raabe, *Peacemaking for Families: A Biblical Guide to Managing Conflict in Your Home* (Wheaton, IL: Tyndale House Publishers, 2002).

Take notice of pleasures that lose their pleasure. When things that you once enjoyed begin to lose their appeal, this should be considered a major red flag. When you do not have the emotional reserve to savor your preferred pleasures, you are likely on the brink of burnout.

Listen to your body. Burnout is not just an emotional experience. Since you are an embodied soul, if something depletes you emotionally it will show up physically. Pay attention if you begin to feel tired often, get sick frequently (sign of lowered immunity), have more frequent headaches or muscle pain, notice changes in your appetite or sleep habits, clinch your jaw when trying to relax, or see signs of digestive problems.

Listen to your emotions. Emotional changes accompany burnout. If you begin to experience (as atypical for you) a loss of motivation, an increase in procrastination, irritability toward lesser stressors, callousness towards problems, or cynicism about life, treat these as probable signs of burnout.

Listen to your family. Your family will probably notice the early warning signs of burnout first. If they say you don't seem like yourself or ask for more time with you, rather than responding to them as if they are criticizing you or calling for you to "do more," consider their concerns about unhealthy changes in your life.

Don't use food or substance to escape. Using food or alcohol to escape stress is like drinking salt water to quench thirst. There is short-term relief, but the problem is actually made much worse.

Connect your work to serving your loving heavenly Father. When work loses purpose, the potential for burnout increases. When work is done as a slave instead of a son, the potential for burnout also increases. Connecting your work with God's service and viewing God as a caring Father is an important balance in preventing burnout.

Multiply yourself in your most demanding responsibilities. If you have areas of your life where there is high demand and few qualified people to which to delegate, a wise line item in your time budget should be toward equipping others to come alongside you.

Listen to how you read your Bible and pray. An exhausted or driven life leads to either neglected or dead Bible study and prayer. If you find yourself bracing against hearing from God because you can't add "one more thing" to your life, then you are probably on the brink of burnout, and your wrong view of God is building your momentum toward collapse.

If you are helping someone whom you fear is on the brink of burnout, you can ask the following questions to discern whether your concern is valid:

- Are you "all there" when you are with your family?
- Do you use your schedule as an excuse for bad eating and sleeping habits?
- Does your devotional time feel rushed, like a checklist item, or get neglected?
- What are your most restorative activities and when do you engage in them?
- When I ask *how* you're doing, why do you tell me *what* you're doing?
- What is your prevailing mood, feeling, or disposition?

THE GOSPEL SOLUTION TO BURNOUT

Practical writings have a strong tendency to only reinforce burnout. This material is no exception. The number of things to do and look for in this material can feed the "do more to get better" mentality that stokes the fires of burnout. As you finish this material, do not consider this final section as a nice devotion to provide closure, but as a vital paradigm shift to effectively apply anything you've read.

As you prepare to contrast your old approach to life with that found in the gospel, consider Hebrews 10:1–14 (bracketed commentary added).[14]

> For since the law [those things I believe I must do to please God, others, and myself] has but a shadow of the good things to come instead of the true form of these realities, it *can never, by the same sacrifices that are continually offered every year, make perfect those who draw near* [here in these words, the exhaustive efforts of people moving toward burnout]. Otherwise, would they not have ceased to be offered, since the worshipers, having once been cleansed, would no longer have any consciousness of sins? *But in these sacrifices there is a reminder of sins every year* [no matter how much we do, it only reminds us what is still to be done]. For it is impossible for the blood of bulls and goats to take away sins.
>
> Consequently, when Christ came into the world, he said, "Sacrifices and offerings you have not desired, but a body have you prepared for me; in burnt offerings and sin offerings you have taken no pleasure. Then I said, 'Behold, I have come to do your will, O God, as it is written of me in the scroll of the book.'"
>
> When he said above, "You have neither desired nor taken pleasure in sacrifices and offerings and burnt offerings and sin offerings" (these are offered according to the law), then he added, "Behold, I have come to do your will." He does away with the first in order to establish the second. And by that will *we have been sanctified through the offering of the body of Jesus Christ once for all* [this should change the motive of everything we do].
>
> And every priest stands daily at his service, offering repeatedly the same sacrifices, which can never take away sins. But when Christ had offered for all time a single sacrifice for sins,

14. I owe the application of Hebrews 10 to burnout to Winston T. Smith from his minibook *Burned Out?*

he sat down at the right hand of God [because Christ is resting in God's presence on our behalf, we can have restful hearts in the midst of our service to him], waiting from that time until his enemies should be made a footstool for his feet. *For by a single offering he has perfected for all time those who are being sanctified.* [This is the guarantee we vainly seek in our performance that leads to burnout.]

The old covenant sacrificial system is an excellent picture of the approach to life that results in burnout. Our duties are offered to God and others day after day, and each morning only reminds us that it all has to be done again. It does not seem like anyone, even God, is pleased for long, because the repetition of life seems to scream, "More! More! More!" For a while we are glad to be able to do something to remedy the problem, but as we master our self-defined "remedy" we only learn how insufficient it is. In a word, it is exhausting—physically, emotionally, mentally, and spiritually exhausting.

Just as the new covenant fulfills the old, it also serves as a picture of what a healthy life without burnout looks like. The old activities are liberated from their futility and slavish demands by the finished work of Christ on the cross. We serve as a response to God's acceptance, rather than trying to gain God's acceptance. We realize that we are not capable or expected to do what only God can do for others in Christ. We accept that our service is only part of God's sovereign ministry to the world around us, and therefore we begin to serve in the freedom which that allows (both emotional and time allocations).

As you seek to apply this material to your life, allow the phrase "restful work" to summarize what you've learned. You can engage your labor with a restful demeanor, because you serve under the care of a loving Father who is fair in his expectations and has guaranteed his desired outcome with the life, death, and resurrection of Christ. Work, rest, and play with the confident hope that the resurrection purchased.